50 Saffron & Smoke: Forgotten Spice Blends

By: Kelly Johnson

Table of Contents

- Ancient Silk Road Saffron Spice Mix
- Phoenician Smoked Date & Cinnamon Blend
- Minoan Olive and Thyme Dust
- Babylonian Sumac & Honey Rub
- Carthaginian Clove & Black Pepper Medley
- Lost Egyptian Frankincense & Anise Blend
- Mesopotamian Barley & Saffron Rub
- Nabatean Myrrh & Cardamom Powder
- Byzantine Bay Leaf & Rose Petal Mix
- Aztec Chili-Cacao Ritual Blend
- Mayan Smoked Vanilla & Annatto Powder
- Viking Birchwood & Sea Salt Rub
- Incan Golden Turmeric & Achiote Blend
- Tang Dynasty Five-Spice Ancestral Dust
- Mughal Empire Saffron & Nutmeg Fusion
- Khmer Tamarind & Lemongrass Spice Rub
- Shang Dynasty Fermented Ginger & Sichuan Blend
- Persian Empire Saffron & Rosewater Mix
- Tibetan Smoked Black Cardamom & Fennel Powder
- Lost Amazonian Urucum & Wild Pepper Mix
- Ottoman Za'atar & Smoked Sumac Blend
- Indus Valley Sesame & Caraway Infusion
- Garamantes Sahara Spice with Date Sugar
- Andalusian Saffron & Smoked Paprika Rub
- Canaanite Coriander & Pomegranate Spice Mix
- Celtic Smoked Heather & Wild Thyme Powder
- Hittite Golden Fennel & Mustard Seed Blend
- Taino Island Citrus & Smoked Peppers Mix
- Ancestral Polynesian Vanilla & Sea Salt Rub
- Mississippian Smoked Corn & Chili Powder
- Harappan Fenugreek & Dried Mango Blend
- Byzantine Cinnamon & Bitter Orange Powder
- Xia Dynasty Black Tea & Star Anise Spice
- Tangierian Almond & Lavender Infusion
- Assyrian Pomegranate & Black Pepper Blend

- Nuragic Sardinian Juniper & Saffron Rub
- Tuareg Frankincense & Smoked Cardamom Mix
- Cahokia Hickory-Smoked Corn & Peppermint Blend
- Lost Khmer Galangal & Kaffir Lime Mix
- Sumerian Fennel & Smoked Honey Dust
- Scythian Wild Thyme & Garlic Infusion
- Garam Masala of the Forbidden Temples
- Nomadic Steppe Fermented Chili & Cumin Mix
- Caral-Supe Amazonian Sweet Bark & Spice Rub
- Atlantean Ocean Salt & Exotic Citrus Blend
- Ethiopian Incense & Coriander Fusion
- Timurid Dynasty Saffron & Clove Medley
- Han Dynasty Smoked Ginger & Cassia Powder
- Aksumite Spiced Coffee Bean & Cardamom Mix
- Hidden Spice of the Alchemists: Saffron & Fire Pepper

Ancient Silk Road Saffron Spice Mix

Ingredients:

- 1 tsp saffron threads
- 1 tbsp ground cinnamon
- ½ tsp ground cloves
- ½ tsp ground star anise
- ½ tsp ground black pepper

Instructions:

1. Gently crush the saffron threads.
2. Mix with all other spices. Store in an airtight container.
3. Use as a rub for meats, rice seasoning, or in stews.

Phoenician Smoked Date & Cinnamon Blend

Ingredients:

- 2 tbsp dried dates, finely ground
- 1 tsp smoked paprika
- 1 tsp ground cinnamon
- ½ tsp nutmeg
- ½ tsp salt

Instructions:

1. Blend ground dates with spices.
2. Store in a dry container.
3. Ideal for roasted meats, stews, or spice-infused bread.

Minoan Olive and Thyme Dust

Ingredients:

- 2 tbsp dried black olives, finely ground
- 1 tbsp dried thyme
- ½ tsp dried oregano
- ½ tsp sea salt

Instructions:

1. Blend all ingredients into a fine powder.
2. Store in an airtight jar.
3. Sprinkle over grilled fish, bread, or vegetable dishes.

Babylonian Sumac & Honey Rub

Ingredients:

- 1 tbsp ground sumac
- 1 tbsp dried honey powder (or fine raw sugar)
- 1 tsp ground coriander
- ½ tsp ground cumin

Instructions:

1. Mix all ingredients and store in a dry place.
2. Great for seasoning lamb, poultry, or roasted vegetables.

Carthaginian Clove & Black Pepper Medley

Ingredients:

- 1 tsp ground cloves
- 1 tsp black peppercorns, crushed
- ½ tsp ground ginger
- ½ tsp dried orange zest

Instructions:

1. Blend all ingredients and store in an airtight container.
2. Use for seasoning meats, spice-infused wines, or stews.

Lost Egyptian Frankincense & Anise Blend

Ingredients:

- ½ tsp ground frankincense resin
- 1 tsp ground anise
- ½ tsp cinnamon
- ¼ tsp ground fenugreek

Instructions:

1. Gently grind frankincense resin into a fine powder.
2. Mix with the rest of the spices.
3. Best used in teas, incense-infused dishes, or slow-cooked meats.

Mesopotamian Barley & Saffron Rub

Ingredients:

- 2 tbsp toasted barley flour
- 1 tsp saffron threads
- 1 tsp ground cumin
- ½ tsp dried mint

Instructions:

1. Toast barley flour until lightly golden.
2. Crush saffron and mix with other spices.
3. Use as a rub for meats or mix into grain-based dishes.

Nabatean Myrrh & Cardamom Powder

Ingredients:

- ½ tsp ground myrrh resin
- 1 tsp ground cardamom
- ½ tsp cinnamon
- ¼ tsp nutmeg

Instructions:

1. Grind myrrh into a fine powder.
2. Mix with the remaining ingredients.
3. Use in aromatic teas, desserts, or as a spice rub.

Byzantine Bay Leaf & Rose Petal Mix

Ingredients:

- 2 dried bay leaves, finely crushed
- 1 tbsp dried rose petals, ground
- ½ tsp ground allspice
- ½ tsp black pepper

Instructions:

1. Crush bay leaves and rose petals into a fine powder.
2. Mix with allspice and pepper.
3. Ideal for seasoning poultry, stews, or spice-infused oils.

Aztec Chili-Cacao Ritual Blend

Ingredients:

- 1 tbsp unsweetened cacao powder
- 1 tsp ground ancho chili
- ½ tsp smoked paprika
- ½ tsp ground allspice
- ¼ tsp cinnamon

Instructions:

1. Blend all ingredients thoroughly.
2. Store in an airtight jar.
3. Use for seasoning meats, mole sauce, or even a spicy hot chocolate.

Mayan Smoked Vanilla & Annatto Powder

Ingredients:

- 1 tbsp annatto powder
- 1 tsp smoked vanilla bean powder
- ½ tsp ground cumin
- ½ tsp ground coriander

Instructions:

1. Combine all ingredients and mix well.
2. Store in a sealed container.
3. Use as a rub for poultry, seafood, or corn-based dishes.

Viking Birchwood & Sea Salt Rub

Ingredients:

- 1 tbsp smoked sea salt
- 1 tsp dried birch bark powder (or substitute with smoked paprika)
- ½ tsp ground juniper berries
- ½ tsp black pepper

Instructions:

1. Grind all ingredients together into a coarse mix.
2. Store in a dry container.
3. Use for curing fish, seasoning meats, or enhancing roasted vegetables.

Incan Golden Turmeric & Achiote Blend

Ingredients:

- 1 tbsp ground turmeric
- 1 tsp achiote powder
- ½ tsp ground coriander
- ½ tsp dried oregano

Instructions:

1. Mix all spices thoroughly.
2. Store in an airtight jar.
3. Ideal for seasoning grains, stews, or roasted meats.

Tang Dynasty Five-Spice Ancestral Dust

Ingredients:

- 1 tsp star anise, ground
- 1 tsp cinnamon
- 1 tsp Sichuan peppercorns, ground
- ½ tsp fennel seeds
- ½ tsp cloves

Instructions:

1. Grind all ingredients together into a fine powder.
2. Store in a dry place.
3. Use for marinades, stir-fries, or roasted duck dishes.

Mughal Empire Saffron & Nutmeg Fusion

Ingredients:

- 1 pinch saffron threads
- 1 tsp ground nutmeg
- ½ tsp cinnamon
- ½ tsp cardamom

Instructions:

1. Lightly crush the saffron threads.
2. Mix with the rest of the ingredients.
3. Best used in rice dishes, stews, or desserts.

Khmer Tamarind & Lemongrass Spice Rub

Ingredients:

- 1 tbsp dried tamarind powder
- 1 tsp dried lemongrass powder
- ½ tsp galangal powder
- ½ tsp black pepper

Instructions:

1. Blend all ingredients into a smooth mixture.
2. Store in an airtight container.
3. Use for fish, poultry, or grilled vegetables.

Shang Dynasty Fermented Ginger & Sichuan Blend

Ingredients:

- 1 tsp dried fermented ginger powder
- 1 tsp ground Sichuan peppercorns
- ½ tsp dried garlic powder
- ½ tsp ground fennel

Instructions:

1. Mix all ingredients together and store in an airtight jar.
2. Use as a spice rub for meats, noodle dishes, or broths.

Persian Empire Saffron & Rosewater Mix

Ingredients:

- 1 pinch saffron threads
- 1 tbsp dried rose petals, ground
- 1 tsp cardamom powder
- ½ tsp cinnamon

Instructions:

1. Crush saffron threads and blend with other spices.
2. Store in a dry container.
3. Use for rice dishes, teas, or desserts.

Tibetan Smoked Black Cardamom & Fennel Powder

Ingredients:

- 1 tsp smoked black cardamom powder
- 1 tsp ground fennel seeds
- ½ tsp nutmeg
- ½ tsp clove powder

Instructions:

1. Mix all ingredients into a fine powder.
2. Store in an airtight container.
3. Perfect for seasoning broths, teas, or slow-cooked dishes.

Lost Amazonian Urucum & Wild Pepper Mix

Ingredients:

- 1 tbsp urucum (achiote) powder
- 1 tsp wild Amazonian black pepper (or substitute with black peppercorns)
- ½ tsp dried lime zest
- ½ tsp ground cumin

Instructions:

1. Blend all ingredients together.
2. Store in an airtight jar.
3. Use for grilled meats, fish, or root vegetable dishes.

Ottoman Za'atar & Smoked Sumac Blend

Ingredients:

- 1 tbsp dried thyme
- 1 tbsp sesame seeds, toasted
- 1 tsp smoked sumac
- ½ tsp ground coriander
- ½ tsp sea salt

Instructions:

1. Toast sesame seeds in a dry pan until golden.
2. Blend all ingredients thoroughly.
3. Store in an airtight container.
4. Use for seasoning meats, vegetables, or flatbreads.

Indus Valley Sesame & Caraway Infusion

Ingredients:

- 1 tbsp toasted sesame seeds
- 1 tsp ground caraway seeds
- ½ tsp black mustard seeds, ground
- ½ tsp dried curry leaves

Instructions:

1. Lightly toast sesame and caraway seeds.
2. Grind into a coarse powder.
3. Store in an airtight jar.
4. Use as a dry rub or in grain-based dishes.

Garamantes Sahara Spice with Date Sugar

Ingredients:

- 1 tbsp date sugar
- 1 tsp ground cinnamon
- 1 tsp ground ginger
- ½ tsp ground cloves
- ½ tsp smoked paprika

Instructions:

1. Blend all ingredients into a fine mixture.
2. Store in a dry, sealed container.
3. Perfect for spicing meats, stews, or teas.

Andalusian Saffron & Smoked Paprika Rub

Ingredients:

- 1 pinch saffron threads
- 1 tbsp smoked paprika
- 1 tsp ground cumin
- ½ tsp black pepper
- ½ tsp sea salt

Instructions:

1. Lightly crush saffron threads.
2. Mix all ingredients together.
3. Store in a dry container.
4. Best for grilled meats, seafood, or paella.

Canaanite Coriander & Pomegranate Spice Mix

Ingredients:

- 1 tbsp ground coriander
- 1 tsp dried pomegranate powder
- ½ tsp sumac
- ½ tsp cinnamon
- ¼ tsp ground anise

Instructions:

1. Blend all ingredients into a smooth mixture.
2. Store in an airtight jar.
3. Use for roasted meats, vegetables, or dips.

Celtic Smoked Heather & Wild Thyme Powder

Ingredients:

- 1 tbsp dried heather flowers
- 1 tsp wild thyme
- ½ tsp smoked sea salt
- ½ tsp crushed juniper berries

Instructions:

1. Grind all ingredients into a fine powder.
2. Store in an airtight jar.
3. Best for seasoning roasted meats or root vegetables.

Hittite Golden Fennel & Mustard Seed Blend

Ingredients:

- 1 tbsp ground fennel seeds
- 1 tsp yellow mustard seeds, ground
- ½ tsp turmeric
- ½ tsp ground bay leaves

Instructions:

1. Toast mustard seeds lightly, then grind.
2. Blend with the remaining ingredients.
3. Store in an airtight jar.
4. Use for seasoning poultry, lentils, or stews.

Taino Island Citrus & Smoked Peppers Mix

Ingredients:

- 1 tbsp dried orange zest
- 1 tsp smoked chili flakes
- ½ tsp ground allspice
- ½ tsp dried oregano
- ½ tsp sea salt

Instructions:

1. Blend all ingredients together.
2. Store in an airtight container.
3. Ideal for marinating seafood, meats, or rice dishes.

Ancestral Polynesian Vanilla & Sea Salt Rub

Ingredients:

- 1 tbsp sea salt
- 1 tsp ground vanilla bean
- ½ tsp coconut sugar
- ½ tsp dried lime zest

Instructions:

1. Mix all ingredients well.
2. Store in a sealed container.
3. Use as a finishing salt for grilled seafood, pork, or tropical desserts.

Mississippian Smoked Corn & Chili Powder

Ingredients:

- 1 tbsp smoked corn powder (finely ground dried corn)
- 1 tsp ancho chili powder
- ½ tsp smoked paprika
- ½ tsp dried oregano
- ¼ tsp sea salt

Instructions:

1. Blend all ingredients into a fine mixture.
2. Store in an airtight container.
3. Use for seasoning grilled meats, stews, or cornbread.

Harappan Fenugreek & Dried Mango Blend

Ingredients:

- 1 tbsp dried mango powder (amchur)
- 1 tsp ground fenugreek seeds
- ½ tsp black salt
- ½ tsp cumin powder

Instructions:

1. Mix all ingredients thoroughly.
2. Store in an airtight container.
3. Ideal for lentils, vegetable curries, or flatbreads.

Byzantine Cinnamon & Bitter Orange Powder

Ingredients:

- 1 tbsp ground cinnamon
- 1 tsp dried bitter orange zest
- ½ tsp ground clove
- ¼ tsp nutmeg

Instructions:

1. Grind the dried orange zest into a fine powder.
2. Mix with the remaining ingredients.
3. Store in a dry, sealed container.
4. Perfect for seasoning desserts, roasted meats, or mulled wine.

Xia Dynasty Black Tea & Star Anise Spice

Ingredients:

- 1 tbsp finely ground black tea leaves
- 1 tsp ground star anise
- ½ tsp ground Sichuan peppercorns
- ¼ tsp cassia bark powder

Instructions:

1. Blend all ingredients together.
2. Store in an airtight container.
3. Best for seasoning duck, pork, or stir-fry dishes.

Tangierian Almond & Lavender Infusion

Ingredients:

- 1 tbsp finely ground almonds
- 1 tsp dried lavender flowers
- ½ tsp ground vanilla bean
- ½ tsp ground coriander

Instructions:

1. Grind the almonds and lavender into a fine powder.
2. Mix with the other ingredients.
3. Store in an airtight container.
4. Ideal for desserts, baked goods, or herbal teas.

Assyrian Pomegranate & Black Pepper Blend

Ingredients:

- 1 tbsp dried pomegranate powder
- 1 tsp freshly ground black pepper
- ½ tsp sumac
- ½ tsp cinnamon

Instructions:

1. Blend all ingredients well.
2. Store in a sealed container.
3. Use for seasoning lamb, poultry, or stews.

Nuragic Sardinian Juniper & Saffron Rub

Ingredients:

- 1 tbsp crushed dried juniper berries
- 1 pinch saffron threads
- ½ tsp sea salt
- ½ tsp ground fennel seeds

Instructions:

1. Grind juniper berries into a fine powder.
2. Blend with saffron, salt, and fennel.
3. Store in an airtight jar.
4. Perfect for game meats, fish, or roasted vegetables.

Tuareg Frankincense & Smoked Cardamom Mix

Ingredients:

- 1 tbsp ground smoked cardamom
- 1 tsp finely ground frankincense resin (food-grade)
- ½ tsp nutmeg
- ½ tsp ground cinnamon

Instructions:

1. Mix all ingredients together.
2. Store in a dry, sealed container.
3. Best for flavoring coffee, teas, or slow-cooked meats.

Cahokia Hickory-Smoked Corn & Peppermint Blend

Ingredients:

- 1 tbsp finely ground hickory-smoked corn
- 1 tsp dried peppermint leaves
- ½ tsp ground allspice
- ¼ tsp smoked salt

Instructions:

1. Blend all ingredients into a fine powder.
2. Store in an airtight jar.
3. Great for seasoning meats, stews, or roasted squash.

Lost Khmer Galangal & Kaffir Lime Mix

Ingredients:

- 1 tbsp dried ground galangal
- 1 tsp dried kaffir lime leaves
- ½ tsp ground lemongrass
- ½ tsp white pepper

Instructions:

1. Grind kaffir lime leaves into a fine powder.
2. Mix with the remaining ingredients.
3. Store in a dry, sealed container.
4. Perfect for curries, soups, or grilled seafood.

Sumerian Fennel & Smoked Honey Dust

Ingredients:

- 1 tbsp ground fennel seeds
- 1 tsp smoked honey powder (or freeze-dried honey)
- ½ tsp ground coriander
- ¼ tsp sea salt

Instructions:

1. Blend all ingredients into a fine powder.
2. Store in an airtight container.
3. Perfect for seasoning roasted meats, bread, or root vegetables.

Scythian Wild Thyme & Garlic Infusion

Ingredients:

- 1 tbsp dried wild thyme
- 1 tsp garlic powder
- ½ tsp ground black pepper
- ¼ tsp dried sumac

Instructions:

1. Grind the thyme into a fine powder.
2. Mix with garlic, black pepper, and sumac.
3. Store in a sealed container.
4. Best for grilled meats, stews, or rustic bread dips.

Garam Masala of the Forbidden Temples

Ingredients:

- 1 tbsp toasted cumin seeds
- 1 tsp ground cinnamon
- ½ tsp ground clove
- ½ tsp ground nutmeg
- ½ tsp ground mace
- ¼ tsp black cardamom powder

Instructions:

1. Toast cumin seeds and grind into a fine powder.
2. Blend with remaining spices.
3. Store in an airtight jar.
4. Ideal for curries, roasted vegetables, or slow-cooked dishes.

Nomadic Steppe Fermented Chili & Cumin Mix

Ingredients:

- 1 tbsp dried fermented chili powder
- 1 tsp ground cumin
- ½ tsp ground black garlic
- ¼ tsp smoked paprika

Instructions:

1. Blend all ingredients together.
2. Store in a dry, sealed container.
3. Best for grilled meats, stews, or dumpling fillings.

Caral-Supe Amazonian Sweet Bark & Spice Rub

Ingredients:

- 1 tbsp ground Amazonian cinnamon (or cassia bark)
- 1 tsp ground annatto seeds
- ½ tsp ground vanilla bean
- ¼ tsp pink sea salt

Instructions:

1. Blend all ingredients into a fine powder.
2. Store in an airtight container.
3. Use for seasoning grilled meats, desserts, or ceremonial cacao drinks.

Atlantean Ocean Salt & Exotic Citrus Blend

Ingredients:

- 1 tbsp flaky sea salt
- 1 tsp dried lemon zest
- ½ tsp dried orange peel powder
- ¼ tsp ground pink peppercorns

Instructions:

1. Blend all ingredients into a fine powder or leave slightly coarse.
2. Store in an airtight container.
3. Sprinkle over grilled seafood, fresh salads, or roasted vegetables.

Ethiopian Incense & Coriander Fusion

Ingredients:

- 1 tbsp ground coriander seeds
- 1 tsp myrrh resin (finely ground)
- ½ tsp smoked paprika
- ¼ tsp ground cinnamon

Instructions:

1. Mix all ingredients thoroughly.
2. Store in an airtight container.
3. Ideal for slow-cooked stews, roasted meats, or Ethiopian-inspired coffee rubs.

Timurid Dynasty Saffron & Clove Medley

Ingredients:

- 1 tbsp ground saffron threads
- 1 tsp ground cloves
- ½ tsp ground nutmeg
- ¼ tsp dried rose petals (powdered)

Instructions:

1. Blend all ingredients together.
2. Store in a sealed container.
3. Best for luxurious rice dishes, Persian-style stews, or spiced desserts.

Han Dynasty Smoked Ginger & Cassia Powder

Ingredients:

- 1 tbsp smoked ginger powder
- 1 tsp ground cassia bark (or cinnamon)
- ½ tsp star anise powder
- ¼ tsp dried Sichuan peppercorns

Instructions:

1. Blend all ingredients into a smooth powder.
2. Store in an airtight container.
3. Use for flavoring stir-fries, braised meats, or traditional Chinese medicinal teas.

Aksumite Spiced Coffee Bean & Cardamom Mix

Ingredients:

- 1 tbsp finely ground Ethiopian coffee beans
- 1 tsp ground green cardamom
- ½ tsp ground cloves
- ¼ tsp ground nutmeg

Instructions:

1. Blend all ingredients together into a fine mix.
2. Store in an airtight container.
3. Ideal for spicing coffee drinks, desserts, or aromatic meat rubs.

Hidden Spice of the Alchemists: Saffron & Fire Pepper

Ingredients:

- 1 tbsp crushed saffron threads
- 1 tsp dried ghost pepper powder
- ½ tsp smoked black salt
- ¼ tsp ground cumin

Instructions:

1. Carefully mix all ingredients.
2. Store in a sealed glass jar.
3. Use sparingly for adding heat and mystery to dishes like stews, roasted meats, or gourmet seafood.